Python Programming:

What EVERY Beginner Needs to Know

Table of Contents

Introduction

I want to thank you and congratulate you on purchasing this book.

This book contains the steps and strategies you will need to become proficient on Python. You may not be adept at Python initially, but by the end of this book, you will master the skills required to run it.

As you navigate these chapters, you will acquire the knowledge base necessary to start using Python as if you knew it well from the very beginning. You will amaze your friends and family with your newfound skills when utilizing this highly lucrative programming language.

Not only that, but you will secure yourself a better job, you will be ahead of your peers, and a more prosperous financial future awaits you as a result. Let's just say you made the right decision by purchasing this book and we commend you for it!!

I truly hope that this will serve as your most useful guide on your journey towards Python mastery. There are many other guides out there that you could have chosen, but you chose this one. And we appreciate that.

Additionally, if you want to master Computer Programming, we have guides on **JavaScript and SQL**. And for anyone interested in surfing the Internet anonymously, we have books on **TOR and Anonymous Internet Surfing.** And finally, no savvy computer user's arsenal would be complete without a basic understanding of **Hacking** (don't worry it's the good kind); so we have books on that fascinating topic as well!!

Check out our Amazon author page to find resources such as this:

If you check out our Programming Library, you WILL increase your earning capacity and marketability at any company dramatically. You will confidently walk into any interview knowing that your skill sets **will be valued** and you have something unique to bring to the table. So don't miss out!!

With that all being said, let's dive into the meat and potatoes of this book. It's time for you to master the Python.

Chapter One:
Python- What Is It and
How Can It Help Me?

Python is a programming language that is widely used and is constantly evolving. The whole purpose behind Python was so that any code that was written within the program was easy to read and the syntax would allow for the programmer to express the concept they are trying to get across in as few lines as possible unlike other programs such as JavaScript or C++.

The interpreters that you find in Python are available on many operating systems so that the program can be run across multiple systems. The great thing about Python is that the download and anything associated with it is free. However, with the system constantly updating, you will have to be sure to go back and check on the Python so that you ensure that you have the most up to date version!

Speaking of using Python, let's get started by downloading it!!

Installing Python

Step one: Step one in being able to *use* Python is downloading Python. You can put Python on any operating system with the click of just a few buttons.

For Windows, the Python interpreter can be found on the Python website for **free**. Before you download the program, you should double check to make sure that you get the version that is appropriate for the system you are using.

You will also need to remember is to download the most up to date version of Python that is available.

For Linux and OS X operating systems that come with Python pre-installed, you will not need to do anything, the most that you will need to download is a text editor.

For most Linux and OS X systems, Python 2.X is still being used. There are some differences between Python 2 and 3, but it is mostly the print statement. However, if you would like to get the newest version of Python for your Linux or OS X system, make sure you go to the Python website to get the appropriate files and the latest update.

Step Two: Make sure that you install the Python interpreter. Most users are able to install the interpreter program without having to change any of their personal settings. If you your options correctly on the list of available modules, you can integrate your version of Python into the Command Prompt that you are using to make things easier to use.

Step Three: It is possible to create Python related programs in programs that are already installed on your system such as Notepad but, it will be easier for you to write programming code in a text editor that is designed for it. Free text editors are available for download such as Notepad++ or, TextWrangler and even JEdit that that is compatible with any system.

Step Four: Now, before you go any further, you'll want to test your installation and make sure it is all working. In order to do this, you need to open the Command Prompt and type in python. From here, python will load, and you will see the version number for the program you are running. Next, you will be taken to the python command prompt which will show up as >>>.

To run your test, type in print ("Hello, Earth!") and then press the enter key. If everything is working properly, the text Hello, Earth! Will be displayed just below the command line.

Learning the basic concepts of Python

Step One: Remember that Python works as an integrated language that will allow you to run any program you create once the changes are made to the selected file. Because of this, python makes it easier to revise and troubleshoot programs quicker some other languages will allow. Since python is one of the more accessible programs to learn, it won't be long before you have a simple program running.

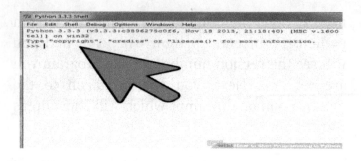

Step Two: If you are testing out how commands work or even writing a program that you are not wanting to keep, you can use the interpreter to test it. The interpreter will allow temporary code without it being added to your program and potentially not working properly.

Step Three: Since python is object oriented, everything you enter is treated just like an object. The good news is that you will not need to declare any of your variables from the start; you are going to be able to add them in at a later. You also do not have to be specific as to what variable you are using.

Using Python as a Calculator

Step One: When opening the Command box, type the word python into the prompt before hitting enter. In doing this, the interpreter will be opened, and you will have the command prompt open in front of you.

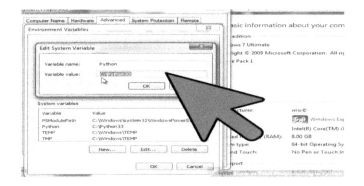

In the case that you did not integrate python into the command, you'll need to go into the python directory to get the interpreter so that it will run.

Step Two: Now that the interpreter is open; you can use python to do basic arithmetic. Note: Should you see # then it means that your code did not go through the interpreter.

Step Three: While using python as a calculator, you can signify powers by using the ** operator. Using this function makes it to where python can quickly calculate any large numbers.

Step Four: You are able to assign variables in python so that python will do basic algebra. Doing this will help you to introduce and assign variables later on. Variables are assigned through the use of the equals (=) sign.

Step Five: After all your calculations are finished, you now need to close your interpreter. In order to do this, you can press Ctrl+Z and then press enter. If you so desire to, you can also type quite () into the command prompt and press enter as well.

Your First Program

Step One: First you'll need to create a test program enables you to use the basics of developing and saving anything that you create with the interpreter. You can also use this as another way to check and make sure that your interpreter is working correctly.

Step Two: "Print" is a primary function that python uses. Print will display its information in the terminal during any programming. Note: "print" was one of the biggest changes to come from python 2 to python 3. While using python 2, you only had to type the word "print" followed by whatever command that you want displayed. But, with python 3, "print" is the same function except you will type your command in different by using print (). Your command will fall between the parentheses.

Step Three: The most common way to test a program is to add in display text. The text "Hello, World!" (That you learned to enter earlier) should be placed within the "print ()" statement and that needs to include the quotation marks.

However, unlike any other programming languages, you do not need to designate when a line ends with a ; Also, you will not need to use {} to denote where blocks are. Instead, you will indent in order to signify what is included in a block.

Step Four: When you are finished, save your file. In order to do this, you will click on the file menu and then click save as (much like if you were trying to save a Word document). In the drop-down menu beneath the name box, you will choose what your python file type is. If you are using regular Notepad, you will select all files and add .py to the file name.

Important: Make sure that you save the file somewhere you can easily find it again later.

Step Five: Reopen your Command Prompt and navigate back to the file in which you placed your file. As soon as you are where you need to be, you will run the file by typing in hello.py, and pressing enter. From here you should see the Hello, World! Displayed beneath your command prompt.

Note: Depending on which version of python you have, there is a possibility that you will have to type the file name in order to run your program.

Step Six: A great thing about using Python as your programming language, you are able to test any new programs instantly. A good idea is to have the command box and editor open simultaneously so that you can test any changes you make immediately.

Building Advanced Programs

Step One: In order to control what a program with specific conditions is a flow control statement. Statements like this are the whole reason behind what python programming does and will enable you to design a program that will do various tasks depending on what you input into it and what your conditions are. The while statement is probably going to be the one that you start with.

Step Two: Any function can be defined and then later called on while in a program. You will find this to be useful when you are using multiple functions inside of a larger program file.

Step Three: As stated previously, control statement will allow for you to set your specific conditions in order to change how a program runs. This will come in handy when prompting user interaction later on.

Step Four: Mathematical symbols such as the less than or greater than symbols are used in python except they are used a little differently.

Step Five: Never stop learning. Go to the Python site and read their documents that they provide for their users. Research any questions that you have on Python and always keep your

Python versions updated and tested to make sure that everything is as it should be.

Why should you learn Python?

Python is going to help you in more aspects than just knowing how to code. There are plenty of jobs out there that use Python and actually have nothing to do with it. You'll learn about that in the next section of this chapter. First, let's briefly analyze why you should learn Python. These are going to be the fundamental reasons as to why you should learn Python.

1. Python is a free language that you can download and learn. This is thanks to the various people who are always trying to improve it and make it better for the next generation of Python users.

2. There are plenty of free resources for learning Python as well. The people who are trying to make Python better have written beginner's guides that are linked to several YouTube videos that are going to help you learn to work Python.

3. Because of how Python is written, it makes for a relatively easy language to learn even for those who have never

played with it before. The program is designed so that the commands you entered are in English and when you tell the computer what to do, all you are doing is writing print and then the command and then the program is going to execute that command. Because of this, you will be able to remember commands easier as well as understand what you are telling the program to do.

4. Many of the websites that you use every day were actually written in Python. For example, Google is written through the coding done in Python and because of that, Google is constantly searching for people proficient and well versed in this language so that they are able to correct corrupted code and build new products.

5. While there are plenty of resources out there that are free for Python, you may want to shell out some money for some of the other books out there. The books that are written by someone who does not work for the Python Foundation are going to have a better structure to them, and they will be easier for you to understand as they are going to have a table of

contents that will tell you what is in the book.

6. Python can be used for programs that are both small and big as well as the ones that are offline and online. It is a program that is completely versatile and is going to be the best option out there for you when you are trying to learn how to code.

7. Python was created with the programmer in mind along with the code; that's why it is so easy and fast to learn.

8. With the help of Python's volunteers, there are new languages constantly coming out for Python, so you never have to worry about it being up to date because it will always be up to date, all you have to do is make sure that you have the proper version installed.

9. There is a huge community of people out there that are just willing to help you with any problem that you may be having with Python. You can find people on twitter, in forums, or even on Facebook that are going to help you with any question that you may have with Python.

How can Python help me?

You've learned a little about what Python is and why you should learn it, but how can learning Python help you in your everyday life? One of the ways is that Python can actually help you get a job or even excel at your current job.

Python can be used to help with certain applications that you may be using in your job. For example, if you work for a software company, you may use Python for text processing. Text processing is going to help you log in files to your database so that you can easily access them and know what you need to do when you need to do it.

Python will also help you when it comes to jobs such as web design and even programming which is a given. With the many functions of Python, you can use it for virtually any job that you could ever want. The only thing is that you will need to learn all of the different modules that Python has to offer in order to use Python for the specification of your job.

Even if your job does not use Python, you may be able to bring it into the workplace so that you can make things easier on yourself and your coworkers. Doing this will demonstrate initiative to your boss and may even earn you a promotion.

Chapter Two:
Python Basics

In order to fully understand how Python works, you must first know the syntax for Python. Since you are new to Python, you do not know about other programming languages. However, if you do, then you are going to notice similarities between Python and programs such as Java or Perl. At the same time, there are some significant differences too.

There are several modes that you must understand when it comes to Python. There is:

- The Interactive Mode

- Script Mode

- Identifier Words

- Reserved Words

- Lines

- Indentations

- Comments

- Quotations

- Multi-line statements

- User interaction

- Suites

- Multi Statements on a single line

- Blank lines

- And the command arguments

Interactive Mode

- The interactive mode is meant to invoke the interpreter without having to falsely set up a parameter by passing the script file as that parameter.

- Because of this, you are going to get the following code:

$ python

Python 2.4.3 (#1, Nov 11 2010, 13:34:43)

[GCC 4.1.2 20080704 (Red Hat 4.1.2-48)] on the Linux 2 system

Type "help," "copyright," "credits" or "license" for more information.

- Now to use Python for what it is meant to be used for. Open a new Python file and type in the following code before you hit enter

Print "Hello, Python!"

- With the newer versions of Python, you will need to put your command inside of a closed set of parenthesis. But, in version 2.4.3 the parenthesis are not going to be required and your output is going to be

Hello, Python!

Script Mode

- When you invoke your interpreter through the use of script parameters so that the script can be executed, the script will then be executed until it reaches the end of the code that has been inputted.

- Once the script is finished, then the interpreter will no longer be active.

- All Python files have the extension of .py

Print "Hello, Python!"

- For this example, we are going to assume that the interpreter has been set to the PATH variable. Try and do this code:

@ python test.py

- From there, your output is going to be

Hello, Python!

- Another example would be:

#!/usr/bin/python

Print "Hello, Python!"

- With this example, it will be assumed that the interpreter is now available inside of your /usr/bin directory. With the location of the interpreter, the code is going to run differently. However you are going to get the same result.

Python Identifiers

- The identifiers that you find in Python are going to be what identifies the various modules, classes, functions, variables, or any other object that needs to be verified.

- The identifier will start with A to Z or even lowercase a to z. There will also be an underscore (_) that is followed usually by a zero or some more letters. The numbers used with an identifier are going to be 0-9.

- There can be no punctuation in the identifiers in Python because it will not allow it.

- Python is case sensitive, so words like Slice and slice are going to have two different meanings.

- An identifier that ends with two trailing underscores is defined as a particular name.

- Class names will start with an uppercase letter. Any other identifier is going to have a lowercase letter.

- When an identifier starts with two leading underscores, then that is an indication of a secure, private identifier.

- When it starts with a single underscore, the identifier will be private.

Reserved Words

- The reserved words will only be used for variables or constants.

- All of the reserved words are going to be lowercased letters.

- And

- Exec

- Not

- Or

- Finally

- Assert

- Break

- For

- Pass

- Print

- From

- Class

- Continue

- Global

- Raise

- Return

- If

- Def

- Del

- Import

- Try

- While

- In

- Elif

- Else

- Is

- With

- Yield

- Lambda

- Except

Lines and Indentation

- Blocks of code are going to be denoted through the indentation on that line

- The variable for indention will be how many spaces it has been indented.

- All statements in a block should be indented the same amount

Example:

if True:

> print "True."

else:

> print "False."

- In this example you will see an error has been found within the code block.

if True:

> print "Answer."

> print "True."

else:

> print "Answer."

> print "False."

- All lines that are continuous will be indented the exact same number of spaces so that a block is formed. (Do not try to understand the coding in this example, it is merely to show you how different blocks have been created through the use of indentions).

Example:

```python
#!/usr/bin/python

import sys

try:

        # open file stream

        File = open(file_name., "w")

except IOError:

        print "There was an error writing to",
file_name

        sys.exit()

print "Enter '", file_finish,

print "' When finished"

while file_text ! = file_finish:

        file_text = raw_input  ("Enter text: ")

        if file_text == file_finish:

                #close the file

                File close.
```

```
                Break

        File.write(file_text)

        File.write("\n")

File.close()

File_name = raw_input ("Enter filename: ")

If len(file_name) == 0:

        Print "Next time please enter something"

        Sys.exit()

Try:

        File = open(file_name, "r")

Except IOError:

        Print "There was an error reading file"

        Sys.exit()

File_text = file.read()

File.close()

Print file_text
```

Multi-line statements

- When statements are written in Python, they are typically ended with a new line.

- Python allows line continuation with the use of a backslash (\) so that the program knows where a line is going to continue.

Example:

Total = item_one + \

    Item_two + \

    Item_three

- If a statement has a set of brackets () [] or {} then the line is not going to have to use a line continuation character since it will already be a given that the line is going to continue.

Example:

Days = ['Monday,' 'Tuesday,' 'Wednesday,' 'Thursday,' 'Friday']

Quotation in Python

- Double ("") and single ('') as well as triple ("""""") quotes are accepted in Python

- Quotes will denote a string just as long as the same quote is used at the beginning and end of the quote.

- Triple quotes are typically used in order to spread the string across a series of lines.

Example:

Word = 'word'

Sentence "This is a sentence."

Paragraph = """ This is a paragraph. It is made up of multiple lines and phrases"""

Comments

- When placing a comment into Python, you will use the hash sign (#)

- Anything that has a # symbol is not going to be executed . Therefore, it is ignored by the program.

Example:

#!/us/bin/python

#first comment

Print "Hello, Python!" #second comment

- Python is still only going to print Hello, Python!

- Comments can be in the same line as an expression or statement.

- Comments can also cover multiple lines

Blank lines

- A blank line is only going to be whitespace which may be a comment

- A blank line is going to be ignored by Python

- For an interpreter that is interactive, then you need to have physically inserted the empty line so that it terminates the multiline statement.

Waiting for User

- Python can be programmed, so that prompts the user to perform a task such as hitting the enter button.

- When the "\n\n" function is used, two lines will be created before the current text.

- As soon as the user hits the key that is required, then the program will be ended.

- This helps to keep a console window open until the application is completed.

Multiple statements on a single line

- Semicolons (;) will allow for multiple statements to be on a single line.

- This can only happen when the statements do not start a new block of code

Example:

Import sys; x = 'foo' ; sys.stdout.write(x + '\n')

Suites

- Groups of individual statements within a single block of code is called a suite.

- Complex or even compound statements will require a header line along with a suite.

- Header lines are going to begin the statement through the use of a keyword and then end with a colon (:)

- These are usually followed by one or more lines to make up the suite.

Example:

If expression :

Suite

Elif expression :

Suite

Else :

Suite

Command line arguments

- Python has a code that is going to tell you how a command should be run.

- In order to access this help, you will type in – h –

Example:

$ python – h

Usage: python [option] ... [-c cmd | -m mod | file | -] [arg] ...

Options and arguments (and corresponding environment variables) :

-c cmd : program passed in as a string (terminates option list)

-d : debug output from parser (also PYTHONDEBUG =x)

-E : ignore environment variables (such as PYTHONPATH)

-h : print this help message and exit.

- There is also the option that your script can be programmed to accept several different options.

39

Chapter Three:
Common Python
Misconceptions

There are a few things that can be found on Python that are not true. some of the coding rules are not necessarily correct either because the program has been updated and that that code is no longer viable, or because the code was not defined correctly in a guide that someone has picked up to use so that they can learn Python.

In this chapter, the misconceptions that you will often find in Python are going to be explained so that you are not making any mistakes that could end up causing you to either lose all of your code that you have created, or to start over from scratch because you are not able to change what you have put into Python.

- When you want to sort your list, you will use the list.sort function. However, this is incorrect. You will actually get a return of none. Your list is not going to be sorted, and you will not be any closer to doing what you wanted to do.

- The is statement does not test for equality in the expression. Instead, it checks to see if the two variables are pointed at the same object.

This works in a lot of cases, however, in other situations, it may not work. The CPython sometimes catches the smaller strings and integers making the underlying objects the same. But, this only happens sometimes. When you want to check if two objects are the same, then you will use == (operators will be discussed in a later chapter.

Example:

In [1]: a = 'hello'

In [2]: b = 'hello'

In [3]: a is b

Out[3]: True

In [4]: a = 'hello world!'

In [5]: b = 'hello world!'

In [6]: a is b

Out[6]: False

In [7]: a = 3

In [8]: b = 3

In [9]: a is b

Out[9]: True

In [10]: a = 1025

In [11]: b = 1025

In [12]: a is b

Out[12]: False

- If you want to do a mutable argument, you will get the same answer. However, there are times that the default argument cannot be evaluated when the function is executed.

As soon as the function is defined, then the default value will have an accurate list that will be empty but is able to be modified.

- Take a look at this code:

X = [1, 2, 3]

For number in x:

Number += 1

Assert (x == [2, 3, 4])

- The number is a reference to the item that you want in the code. The int will be immutable, and the += is going to assign a new value to the name that you have put in. therefore, the values within the list are going to be unchangeable.

Chapter Four:
Mistakes and How to
Avoid Them

As a beginner you are going to make mistakes, there is no way around it. But, if you know some of the more common mistakes that you can make, and how you are going to be able to avoid them, then you will be able to make different mistakes and learn from them. Even if you do make one of these mistakes, you are going to have it easier than someone who did not pick up this book because they are not going to know how to correct the error if it happens to them.

- Data Types: as you go through Python, you will have access to an extensive database of data types. The most common mistake with data types is to execute your query before the developer has time to go through all of the data types and choose the right one.

There is an overview of data types can be found on the Python website so that you are able to go through and learn the various data types.

- Reinvention: when you are learning Python, you can end up "reinventing the wheel" by going into the primary methods and changing them to try and make them easier. The methods that are already in place should be left alone because they are there for a reason. Because they work!

- Do not try and use Python for analyzing big data loads. Python was made for analyzing small data loads. If you want to do a larger set of data, then you are going to need to use a third-party framework.

- The misuse of an expression for a default for function arguments: as you work with Python, you will see that it allows you to choose if you want to specify your argument or by just selecting the default option. Some confusion can come when your default value become mutable.

Some people think that the optional argument is going to specify a default expression every time that it is called upon even if a value is not provided for the optional argument.

In order to fix this, you are going to want to have the default value only be evaluated once when the function is defined. This is going to continue with the same list instead of creating a new one.

- Using class variables incorrectly: The class variables will be internally handled by the dictionaries and only follow the MRO (Method Resolution Order). When this happens, the program is going to try and manage the problem correctly. To avoid this, you are going to need to make sure that every variable has its own property.

- Specifying parameters incorrectly for an exception block: when a statement does not take to the exceptions that are accepted by Python, it is not defined in the correct manner. Therefore, the syntax is going to bind the exception to the second parameter that is optional in order to make it available to be inspected further.

Because of this, the exception is not going to be caught by the except statement. Instead, the exception is bound to a different parameter. To correct this mistake, then you are going to need to find the various exceptions to the statement so that you can make sure they are specified in the first parameter as the tuple so that all exceptions are caught.

Also, use the as keyword so that the syntax is supported in both Python 2 and 3.

Chapter Five:
Python Strategies

When you are using Python, it can seem a little confusing at first. There are so many different things that you have to remember about how a code goes into the program and then how it is to be executed. But, there are some strategies that you can use to try and remember what it is that you need to be doing.

These procedures are meant to help make starting out with Python easier without getting in over your head and feeling as if learning Python is a helpless cause, because it's not!

- When you first open Python, there are going to be lines of various code. This code is either the code that you have put in yourself as you have been playing with it, or it is code that was put into Python by the program.

- First, have Python type back the words that you put into Python. The ">>>" is going to tell you the program is prompting you to type in the codes and commands that you want to enter into Python. For example, when you enter print "Hello, my lover!" Then your output is going to be what you typed in, without the quotation marks.

- Python can act as your calculator. If you enter print "5", your output will just be the number 5. But, if you enter in print "20+98" then your output will be 118.

- While you are going to be able to get Python to give you back what you put into it, and you will be able to use Python as a calculator, but you cannot mix the two together.

For example, if you were to enter print "I am Superman + 2315" then an error code is going to be given to you because what you are trying to do is not plausible through Python. So, your error code will look a little something like this:

Traceback (most recent call last)

File "<pyshell#6>", line1, in <module>

Print "I am Superman +2315."

TypeError: cannot concatenate 'str' and 'int' objects.

- Whenever you see the word "file", it is telling you which file the error is occurring in. After that, you will see the code and a short description of what the error code is. For this example, the error code was telling you that you cannot place strings and integers together.

- In order to get around this error, you are going to have to put in a different code that means the same thing, but it is going to be a different code so that the program does not see numbers and letters in the same expression.

- The first step in getting around the error code is to remember your math. X was always used as a placeholder and will be now. So, you will put your number for x. In this example, X will be 2315.

- Next, you will enter in your code just as you did earlier, however, you are not going to put your numbers in. Therefore, your code is going to look like this: print "I am Superman + X.

- **Do not hit enter!** If you do, then you are going to receive the exact same error code.

- At this point in time, you will need to change the variable for X so that it is now a string through the use of quotation marks and apostrophes.

X = '2315'

Print "I am Superman + X

- Now, when you hit enter, your code is going to read like this. I am Superman 2315.

Dict/Set Comprehension

Later in this book, we will discuss lists and the comprehension of those lists. However, there is also dicts and sets that are able to be comprehended as well as you are using Python.

- Dicts and sets are simple to use and just as effective as a list comprehension

- Dicts and sets are just like a list except they are going to be a mathematical equation of sorts where the variable is going to fall within a particular range.

For example:

My_dict = {i: i*i for i in xrange(100)}

My set = {i * 15 for i in xrange(100)}

- The biggest difference between a dict and a set is that a set is going to have the colon (:) before the equation.

Forcing Float Division

- Numbers in Python can be divided with the backslash (\) key.

- Generally, Python will give you an output of a whole number, however, in Python 2, the answer is going to be different because the equation is going to be different.

Example: 1.0/2

- You are able to forgo the .0 through the use of code manipulation.

The code is:

From_future_import division

Result = ½

print(result)

0.5

- With Python 3 though, this problem has been fixed, and Python automatically handles the division the way that it is supposed to be handled.

Chapter Six:
Variables

When looking at the variables in Python, you need to know that they are simply there to reserve a location that you will late store values in. Therefore, when you are creating a variable, you need to make sure that you save a little bit of space in the memory for the value.

Depending on the data type that you are working with is going to determine whether the interpreter is going to allow the memory to be saved as well as deciding what is going to be stored in the memory reserve.

The different data types that are assigned to the various variables are going to let you store characters, integers, and even decimals into the variable.

Assigning Values to Variables

- Your variable is not going to need to have expressed permission to reserve space on the memory. This permission is granted whenever a value is assigned to the variable.

- In order to assign the value, you are going to use the equals sign (=)

- Everything that is on the left of the equals sign is going to be the variable

- Everything on the right is going to be the value that has been stored in the variable.

- As you are assigning the proper value to the variables, then you will need to be sure that you are putting the correct value in the right place.

Example:

Age = 23

Year = 1994

Name = Susan

- The variables in this example are the age, year, and name of the user. 23, 1994, and Susan are the values that are assigned to those variables.

Multiple Assignment:

- The same value can be assigned to different variables thanks to Python.

- If you want to assign the number 5 to the letters x, y, and z, you will be able to!

- The integer is going to have the same memory location despite the fact that it is assigned to multiple variables.

Standard Data Types

- The data that you need to store into the memory is going to come in many different types.

- The data that is inputted is going to depend on which data type it will fall under. For example, age may stored as a numeric value while an address may be stored as alphanumeric characters.

- Data types are also used to define the operations that can be done within that data type along with how the values are going to be stored.

- These five data types are the data types that you are going to run into the most when you are using Python (They will be discussed in more detail further in the book).

  o Dictionary

  o Numbers

  o String

  o Tuple

  o List

Chapter Seven:
Mathematical Operators

As mentioned earlier. You can use Python as a calculator even for the more advanced mathematics such as trigonometry. However, when you look at the different ways that you can use Python for math, you are going to need to remember that the operator is going to be the manipulator for the values that are placed on the operands.

If you have the expression of 2+5=7, then your operands are going to be 2 and 5 while the plus sign is the operator.

- Python supports a variety of different operators that you are going to be able to use in order to do your math correctly.

  o Identity operators

  o Logical operators

  o Arithmetic operators

  o Assignment operators

  o Membership operators

o Comparison operators

o Bitwise operators

Comparison Operators

- The comparison operator is going to compare the values that you find on either side of the operator and determine their relationship.

- Comparison operators are also known as relational operators.

- == will describe the values of being equal while the condition is true.

- <> is going to say that the operands are not equal, but the condition is true.

- != the values will not be equal but the condition will be true.

- > the value found on the left is greater than the value on the right.

- < the value on the right is less than the value on the right.

- <= the value found on the left is less than or equal to the value found on the right.

- >= the operand on the left is greater than or equal to the value that you find on the right.

Arithmetic Operators

The basic mathematical operators that you did in Elementary school are going to be the same ones that you are going to use for Python. Except, there are a few other ones that you will use that are not going to be like the ones that you did in school.

- Modulus is represented by the percentage sign (%), and this is going to divide the left from the right before returning a remainder to you.

- Exponents are represented through two asterisks (**) and will perform the exponential on both of the operands.

- Floor division will use a double backslash (\\) and is going to divide both numbers so that the result is a remainder of a decimal.

Assignment Operators

- The assignment operators are going to take one value and do an arithmetic operation to it before assigning it to one side or the other.

- Usually, the answer that you get from your operation is going to be attached to the left side.

Bitwise Operators

- The bitwise is going to work with bits while executing the process bit by bit.

- Answers for bitwise are going to be in binary code

- & AND will copy the operator so that each operand has the same results.

- | OR is going to copy the bit that is only existent on either of the operands.

- ^ XOR will copy the bit should it exist on one set of operands, but it cannot exist on both sets.

- ~ A Binary One's Complement is going to flip the bits

- << When a left shift happens based on how many bits are on the right, it is known as a Binary Left Shift.

- >> Binary Right Shift occurs when the operand moves right based on the number of bits on the right operand.

Identity Operators

- An identity operator is going to compare the location of two objects on based on where they are located in the memory.

- The statement will be true should the variables point at the same object that can be found on either side of the operator. If they do not point to the same object, then the statement is going to be false.

- The statement will also be true if the subject matter of either operator points to the same object.

Membership Operators

- The membership operator will test the membership of a sequence such as a list.

- The evaluation is going to be true when a variable is found within the individual sequence. However, it will be false should the variable not be in the proper sequence.

- If the variable is not in the proper place, then the other variations of this sequence are going to be false as well.

Operators Precedence

- The operations in this list are from the highest priority to the lowest

- ** will raise the operand to the power of x

- ~+- the complement will be done first before the unary plus and finally everything will be subtracted.

- */%// multiplication will be done first before you divide it. Next will come the modulo and finally you will finish it off with the floor division.

- +- addition and subtraction will be done to the operands.

- >> << the left and right shift because of the bitwise.

- & AND

- ^| OR

- <= << >> = comparison operator

- < > == ! = equality operator

- = % = / = // = - = + = * = ** = assignment operator

- Is is not are identity operators

- In not in are considered membership operators

- Not or and are the logical operators

Chapter Eight:
Common Data Types

Numbers

- A numeric value is going to be stored under the numbers data type.

- Numerics are immutable, so they cannot be changed once they have been created.

- There are three main numerics that you will use as you code in Python

  o Floating Point Numbers

  o Complex Numbers

  o Integers

- A complex number is mostly used when you are doing engineering.

- Complex numbers have imaginary numbers so your form for a complex number will usually be A+Bi

- Python will support a complex number whether it has real or imaginary numbers.

- Your functions will either be real+imagJ or real+imagj.

- Python also has a built in function that will work for complex numbers through the use of (x, y)

Strings

- Strings are one of the most popular data types that you will use in Python.

- A string is going to be read from left to right just like you would read anything else.

- Strings will start out with quotes either single or double

- They are immutable meaning that they cannot be changed once they have been created.

- The quotes that start and end a string can be interchanged and the string will still be executed as it is supposed to be.

For example:

"Hello, Destiny"

'Hello, Destiny'

- Both will be executed to print out Hello, Destiny without the quotation marks.

- Do not mix and match quotes. If you start with double quotes, then you must end with double quotes. Doing this will give you an error code.

- A single backslash is used in order to introduce a new character to the string.

    o \" is going to put a double quote into the string

    o \n will start a new line

    o \' a single quote will be entered into the string

    o \t will move the line on a horizontal axis.

    o \\ is going to give you a backslash in the string.

- Any character or element that is in your string can be accessed through your index.

- If you put in the code print "Python Tutorial", you will get a tutorial on how to create strings in Python.

- Your index is going to have positive numbers starting on the right and negative numbers on the left. The negative numbers are going to start with a larger number than the positive ones did.

- Double check your work before you hit enter on your string because you will not be able to correct it if you have made a mistake once it has been created.

- The "in" operator will allow you to determine if the substrings and characters are going to be inside of your string or not. Usually, a Boolean value will be returned after this has been executed.

- Cutting a substring out of the string means that you will need to separate the two indexes through the use of a colon (:).

- Should you want to slice your string between 3 and 8, you will enter 3:8 into Python and then the string will be spliced three to seven.

List

- With a list, every object is going to be separated by commas while being contained within a closed set of square brackets.

- As you create your list, you are going to use the same function that is used for placing anything into Python. The only difference will be that you will put your elements for your list between parentheses.

- To start a list from scratch, you will enter the function print(my_list) so that you can make your list from scratch.

- Your list is going to have an index just like a string will have.

- The index for your list is going to duplicate that of the string.

- List indexes are color coated with blue, red, green, and black.

- An index value that is out of range is going to return an error message because of the interpreter that is being used.

- Lists can be spliced by using the function sliced_list = List_Name [startIndex: endIndex]

- The objects being sliced are going to start where you have chosen and end just before the end index.

- The default value is always going to be zero

- If you want to slice the original list that you have created, then you will omit the beginning and ending indexes

- Lists are mutable so they can be changed even after you have pressed enter and created it.

- A plus (+) sign is going to create a new list that will still be connected to the previous list that you have created.

- An asterisk (*) is going to repeat the list that you have chosen.

Dictionaries

- Dictionaries are a set of unordered objects

- The objects in a dictionary are surrounded by the curly braces ({}).

- A dictionary separates different items and valued pairs with the use of a comma.

- The values and keys are data types.

Chapter Nine:
Tuples and Lists

Lists

- The list that you create is going to have variables listed on it that are named after objects that you choose in order to help you to remember them later.

- Python keeps track of any data types that you use.

- Lists are useful for many things depending on the code that you have used to create it.

List Codes

- List.reverse(): the elements located on the list will be reversed.

- List.append(x): an item will be added to the end of the list

- List.insert(I, x): an element can be inserted into a specified spot on the list.

- List.extend(L): the list can be extended by appending all of the objects that are currently located on your list.

- List.pop([i]): an item can be returned to the list before it is removed. If a particular spot is not indicated, then the item will be placed in the last position on the list.

- List.index(x): returns the index to the first item. An error indicates that the object you are looking for does not exist.

- List.sort(cmp = non, key= non, reverse = false): the arguments within your list will be sorted.

- List.count(x): tells the number of times that any particular value appears in your list.

Example:

A – [62.3, 255, 255, 2, 6.5432]

Print a.count(255), account(62.3), a.count('x')

3 2 0

a.insert (3, -5)

```
a.append(255)
a
[62.3, 255, -5, 255, 5, 6.5432, 255]
a.indes(255)
5
a.remove(255)
a
[62.3, 255, -5, 255, 5, 6.5432]
a.reverse()
a
[255, 6.5432, 5, 255, -5, 62.3]
a.sort()
a
[-5, 5, 62.3, 255, 255, 6.5432]
a.pop()
6.5432
a
```

[-5, 5, 62.3, 255, 255]

Tuple

- As the standard data type in Python, tuples are never going to change, no matter how much Python evolves.

- A tuple is a set that contains values that will be numbered and separated by commas.

Example:

>>> t = 23456, 65432, 'hi!'

>>> t[0]

23456

>>> t

(23456, 65432, 'hi!')

>>> # tuples have the ability to be nested

... u = t, (2, 3, 4, 5, 6)

>>> u

((23456,65432, 'hi!'), (2, 3, 4, 5, 6))

- The output from a tuple will need to be within closed parentheses in order to be nested properly.

- When a tuple is nested properly, then the tuple will be interpreted correctly.

- A nest tuple is going to be inputted into Python without brackets

- Parentheses are a must when working with larger expressions.

- A tuple can be used in order track things such as employee records.

- Tuples are immutable.

- A tuple has a few quirks that have been covered up thanks to certain little characteristics that have been put into place to correct the problems.

- An empty tuple can be created through the use of parentheses left empty.

- In the event that a tuple has just one item, that item is still going to be followed by a comma.

- Because there is only one item, it does not have to be closed off.

- The code may end up looking ugly to some, but this is the best way to write it.

Example:

>>> empty = ()

>>> singleton = 'hi'. # ← a trailing comma

>>> len(empty)

0

>>> len(singleton)

5

>>>singleton

('hi',)

- A t statement can be represented by the numbers 23456, 65432, hi!

- When you do this, you are doing what is known as tuple packing.

- Tuple packing is when the values and characters are in the same tuple

- Tuples have the ability to be reversed by using x, y, z = t

- Just as tuples can be packed, they can be unpacked.

- To unpack a tuple, you must have the same amount of variables on the left as the number of objects that you have entered into the tuple.

- If there are multiple assignments, the tuple has to be packed and then unpacked.

- There may be the occasional operation that corresponds in order to make unpacking more useful.

- Unpacking the tuple is supported through the variables that are inside of the square brackets.

Example

>>> a ['leaves , 'snickers', 500, 5678]

>>> [a1, a2, a3, a4] = a

Chapter Ten:
String Formatting

- Strings have different constants and will contain various classes that will end up being useful

- Strings can have legacy functions that you will only find when you are creating strings.

- The string types that you find in Python will support sequencing type methods.

- The output from the strings can be formatted. A templet can be used or the percentage sign will do the same thing.

- A built-in tool can be used in order to help with the formatting of strings.

- The Unicode as well as the str classes have been placed into Python so that there is help with complex variables when using the str.format() function.

Formatting code

- Format(format_string, *args, **kwards): this is the API method that is used most often. You can format your string through the use of random keywords and the position that they hold.

- Get_field(field_name, args, kwargs): the field name will be returned by using parse(). By using this, you will need to convert your object in order for it to be formatted correctly.

- Parase(format_string): the objects in your string are going to be formatted after they have been converted into a tuple.

- Get_value(key, ,args, kwards): the field value is going to be retrieved as long as you keep it inside of the list.

- Check_unused_args(used_args, args, kwards): the arguments that you use have to be checked so that you are not using them again. The arguments that you have set up will refer to the strings that have previously been formatted.

- Format_field(value, format_spec): the format() function is a global function. This method is going to override any sub classes.

- Convert_field(value, conversion): the value will be returned before it is converted. Default versions will be repr(r), str(s), and asci(a).

Chapter Eleven:
Modules and Functions

The cool thing about modules and functions is that they are going to be predefined in Python. While they work on a similar level, there are different variations of a function and a module.

Modules

- Modules are files that have definitions and statements from Python.

- The file name usually ends in .py, but the module name is a string that is open because of the value of the global variable.

- The file name is going to be whatever you choose to name it.py so ultimately it will be name.py

- Should the Python interpreter be quit, then all of the work that you have done will be gone.

- It is recommended that you save all of your work in a different program such as Notepad.

- Inputting a different file into Python is known as scripting. This ensures that your work is being saved so that you do not lose it because you do not have the time to sit and do the coding all in one setting.

- Longer programs should be broken up into multiple files. This is to ensure that you catch all mistakes before you enter it into Python.

- The statements and definitions that you have used previously with Python will be executed properly.

Module example:

```
#Fibonacci numbers module

Def fib(n) : # write Fibonacci series up to n

        A, b  = 0, 1

        While b < n:

                Print b,

                A, b = b, a+b

Def fib2(n) : # return Fibonacci series up to n

        Results = [ ]

        A, b = 0, 1

        While b < n:

                Result . append(b)

                A , b = b, a+b

        Return result
```

- The module will be imported with the fibo command.

- After it has been identified, then it cannot be entered into Python however, it will create the module

- Once it has been created, all functions will be accessible.

Functions

- Functions are defined through Python syntax.

Example:

Def functionname (arg2, arg2, …):

Statement 2

Statement 3

Etc.

- If an object is callable, then it is accepted inside of a limited number of arguments that are otherwise known as parameters.

- Your return will be the possibility of the object being a tuple in order to have multiple objects.

- When a function does not have parameters, it will be contained within a set of parentheses. But, there will be nothing between them.

Example:

Def functionname()

Statement 2

Statement 3

Etc.

Chapter Twelve:
Loops

- General statements are usually executed sequentially. Meaning, the first statement is going to be executed first, the second, second and so on in that order.

- There are some situations that are going to cause a block of code to be executed several times.

- Programming languages are meant to provide some control structures so more complicated execution paths are allowed.

- The loop will allow for a statement or group of statements to be executed numerous times.

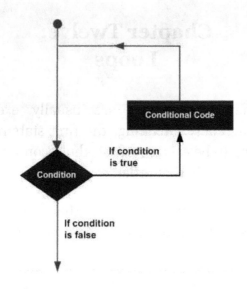

- Python allows for various loop types in order to handle the looping requirements set forth by Python.

Loop Types

- Nested loops: you can use one or more loops inside of another.

- While loop: repeats a statement if the condition is true.

- For loop: executes the sequence of statements while abbreviating the code in order to manage the loop variable.

Loop Control Statements

- The control statements will change the normal execution

- Execution will leave a scope so that all automatic objects that have been created are going to be destroyed.

Control statements

- Pass statement: the statement is required syntactically however; you are not going to want a command or code to execute

- Break statement: the loop statement will be terminated and transferred to the statement that follows the loop

- Continued statement: the loop will skip the remainder and immediately retest the condition prior to reiterating.

Chapter Thirteen:
Decision Making

- The decision making process will anticipate the conditions that occur while the program is executing the code and specifying the actions that have been taken in accordance to the conditions.

- The decision structures are going to evaluate various expressions in order to get an outcome of true or false.

- It is up to you to determine the action that will be taken and which of the statements will be executed should the outcome be true or false otherwise.

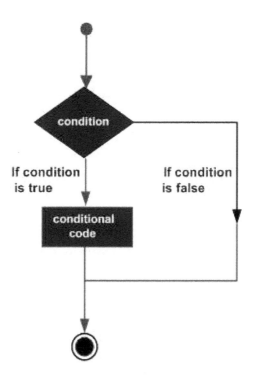

- Python assumes that there are non-zero and non-null values that will be true.

- If it is just zero or null, then it is going to be assumed as a false value.

Decision Making Statements

- Nested if statements: you are able to use one if or else if inside of another if or else if statement.

- If statements: if statements contain a Boolean expression before being followed by one or more statements

- If...else statements: the if statement is going to be followed by an else statement that will execute if the Boolean expression is deemed as false.

Single Statement Suites

- The suite in an if clause is going to consist of a single line.

- The same line may have a header statement.

Example:

```
#!/usr/bin/python

Var = 100

If (var ==100) : print "Value of expression is 100"

Print "Good bye!"
```

After the code has been executed then you are going to get the output:

Value of expression is 100

Good bye!

Chapter Fourteen:
Exceptions

- There are two features that you are going to use in order to handle any error that happens unexpectedly in Python. These functions also have debugging capabilities in them.

    o Assertions

    o Exception handling

Standard Exceptions

- Exception: this is the base class for any and all exceptions in Python

- SystemExit: this is raised because of the sys.exit() function

- StopIteration: the next() method is going to be raised when the iterator does not have an object to point to.

- StandardError: the base class for any exception that has been built-in except for the StopIteration and SystemExit

- ArithmeticError: the base class for any error that occurs inside of a numeric calculation

- OverflowError: this is raised whenever the calculation has exxeded the maximum limit for the numeric type.

- FloatingPointError: When a floating point calculation fails the execution

- ZeroDivisionError: When the division or modulo is done by zero. This can be done to all numeric types

- AssertionError: the case failure for an Assert statement

- AttributeError: the case of failure for an attributed reference or assignment.

- EOFError: when there is no input from the input() or raw_input()

- ImportError: Raised when the import statement fails

- KeyboardInterrupt: the user will interrupt the program's execution normally by pressing Ctrl+c

- LookupError: the base class of any lookup error

- IndexError: the index cannot be found inside of the sequence

- KeyError: the specified key cannot be found in the directory.

- NameError: the identifier cannot be found in the local or global namespace.

- UnboundLocalError: when access to the local variable is tried and there has been no variable assigned to it.

- EnviromentError: the base class for any exception that occurs outside of the environment created by Python.

- IOError: the input/output operation will fail such as the print statement or the open() function because the file does not exist. It also is related to the operating system errors.

- SyntaxError: when there is an issue with the syntax.

- IndentationError: when an indentation is not specified properly.

- SystemError: the interpreter finds a problem internally, but the error finds that the interpreter does not exist.

- SystemExit: when the interpreter is quit because of the sys.exit() function

- ValueError: the function that is built in for the data type has valid type for the arguments, but the arguments do not have valid values specified.

- RuntimeError: the error does not fall into any category.

- NotImplementedError: the abstract method has to be implemented with an inherited class that has not been implemented.

Assertions in Python

- The assertion is a sanity check of what can be turned on or off when the testing of a program has been done.

- An assertion statement should be thought of as a raise-if statement.

- The expression will be tested and the result may come up false. If this happens, then an exception will be raised.

- Assertions are normally carried out with an assert statement.

- Programmers place assertions at the beginning of a function in order to check for a valid input and output.

The Assert Statement

- When an assert statement has been encounter, Python will evaluate the expression to see if it is true.

- Should the statement end up false, then Python will raise the AssertionError exception.

Example:

Assert Expression[, Arguments]

- If the assertion fails, then the ArgumentExpression is gong to be the argument that is put into place for the AssertionError.

- AssertionError exceptions will be handled like any other exception, by using the try-except statement

- If it is not handled, then the program will be terminated while producing a traceback

Example:

When a function converts Kelvin degrees to Fahrenheit. The coldest it gets in Kelvin is zero degrees. The function will bail if a negative temperature is inputted.

```
#!/usr/bin/python

Def KelvinToFahrenheit(Temperature):

Assert (Temperature >= 0_, "Colder than absolute zero!"

Return ((Temperature -273) * 1.8)+32

Print KelvinToFahrenheit(273)

Print int (KelvinToFahrenheit(505.78))

Print KelvinToFahrenheit(-5)
```

After the code has been executed, your output is going to look like this:

32.0

451

Traceback (Most recent call last):

File "test.py", line 9, in

Print KelvinToFahrenheit(-5)

Assert (Temperature >= 0), "Colder than absolute zero!"

AssertionError: Colder than absolute zero!

What is an Exception?

- The exception is going to be an event where the exception is executed form the program that disrupts the programs normal flow of instructions.

- Python scripts encounter situations where it cannot cope and then an exception is raised.

- After an exception is raised, the object is going to represent an error.

- Python's script has to hand the expectation immediately after it has been raised or it will be terminated.

Handling an Exception

- When suspicious code is in the system, then an exception is going to be raised. The program can be defended by placing that suspicious code into a try block.

- The try block is going to include an exception that is followed by a block of code so that the problem is handled as elegantly as possible.

Syntax

Example

Try:

You do your operations here;

Except ExceptionI:

If there is ExceptionI, then execute this block.

Except ExceptionII:

If there is ExceptionII, then execute this block.

Else:

If there is no exception then execute this block.

- Some important things that you should remember are:

- The try statement that is single can end up having multiple except statements. You will find this useful when the try block has statements that can throw out different types of exceptions.

- Generic except clauses will also hand any exception

- After an except clause there can be an else clause. The code that is in the else block is going to be executed like the code in the try block that did not raise the exception.

- An else block is going to be the place that the code will not need to be tried. This is for the block's protection.

Example:

If a file is opened and then has consents written into it, the file is going to come out gracefully since there is not going to be any problem.

```
#!/usr/bin/python

Try:

Fh = open("testfile", "w")

Fh.write ("this is my test file for exception handling!!")

Ecept IOError

Print "Error: can\'t find finle or read data"

Else:

Print "Written content in the file successfully

Fh.close()
```

The outcome for the following code is going to be:

Written content in the file successfully

Another example:

The program tries to open a file but you do not have the permission to edit this file, so an exception is going to be raised.

```
#!/usr/bin/python

Try:

Fh = open("testfile", "r")

Fh.write("this is my test file for exception handling!!")

Except IOError:

Print "Error: can\'t find file or read data"

Else:

Print" Written content in the file successfully"
```

The outcome is:

Error: can't find file or read data

The *Except* Clause with No Exceptions

- Except statements that have no exceptions are defined like this:

Try: you do your operations here;

Except:

If there is any exception, then execute this block

Else:

If there is no exception, then execute this block.

The try-finally Clause

- A finally block can be used along with a try block.

- The final block is going to put any code that has to be executed whether the try block has an exception or not.

Example:

Try:

You do your operations here;

Due to any exception, this may be skipped

Finally:

This would always be executed.

- The else clause cannot be used with a finally clause

Example:

```
#!/usr/bin/python

Try:

Fh=open("testfile", "w")

Fh.write("this is my test file for exception
handling!!")

Finally:

Print "Error: can\'t find file or read data"
```

- When you do not have the permission needed to open a file to edit it, the your output will be:

Error: can't find file or read data

- To have a code that is written more clearly, it is going to look like this.

```
#!/usr/bin/python

Try:

Fh = open("testfile", "w")

Try:
```

Fh.write ("this is my test file for exception handling!!")

Finally:

Print "Going to close the file"

Fh.close()

Except IOError

Print "Error: can\'t find file or read data"

- Whenever an exception is put into the try block, then the execution is going to be passed immediately to a finally block

- Any statement in a finally block will be executed

- The exception that is raised again is going to be handled by the except statement should it be present in than next layer for the try-except statement.

Argument of an Exception

- The exception can have an argument to give the value some additional information about the current problem.

- The contents of the argument are going to vary based on the exception.

- An exception can be captured by the argument by supplying the variable in the except clause.

Example:

Try:

You do your operations here;

Except ExceptionType, Argument:

You can print value of Argument here...

- The code can be written to handle a single exception. The variable that follows the name of the exception will be in the except statement.

- When trapping multiple exceptions, the variable will follow a tuple of the exception.

- The variable will receive the value for the exception that contains most of the cause from the exception.

- The variable is going to receive the value of the exception which is going to contain the clause from the exception.

- The variable is able to be receive a single value or even multiple values if in the form of a tuple.

- The tuple is most likely going to contain a error string, error location, and even error number.

Example:

#!/ usr/bin/python

#define a function here

Def temp_convert(var):

Try:

Return in(var)

Except ValueError, Argument:

Print "the argument does not contain numbers\n", Argument

#Call above function here.

Temp_convert ("xyx");

The following result is going to be

The argument does not contain numbers

Invalid literal for int() with base 10: 'xyz'

Raising an Exception

- Exceptions can be raised through the use of a raise statement.

- The general syntax for this statement will be:

Raise [Exception [, args [, traceback]]]

- The exception is going to be a specific type of exception as well as the argument being a value for the exception argument.

- The argument is going to be optional. If you do not supply it, the exception argument will be none.

- The finale argument and traceback are also optional and hardly ever used when practicing with Python. If it is presene,t then the traceback is going to be used for the exception.

Example

The exception will be a string, class, or object. Many exceptions that Pyhon's core raises are going to be classes that contain an argument that will be an instance of the class. When defining new exceptions, it is easy and will be done like this:

Def function Name(level):

If level < 1:

Raise "Invalid level!", level

#The code below to this would not be executed

#if we raise the exception

- Keep in mind that to catch an exception, the except clause will refer to the same exception that is placed on class, object, or a simple string.

Example

Try:

Business logic here...

Except "Invalid level!":

Exception handling here....

Else:

Rest of the code here...

User-defined Exceptions

- Python will allow the user to create exceptions through deriving classes that are built in to the standard exceptions

Example:

Class Networerror (RuntimeError):

Def_init_(self, arg):

Self.args = arg

- Once the classes have been defined, the exception will be like this:

Try:

Raise Networkerror ("Bad hostname")

Except Networkerror, e:

Print e.args

Chapter Fifteen:
Date and Time

- When working with Python, you are going to be able to get the date as well as the time in several different ways.

- Converting between the different date formats is going to be a chore for any computer.

- Python's time and calendar was made to keep track of the dates and time with very little effort.

What is a Tick?

- The time intervals will be floating point numbers with units for seconds.

- A particular instant in time will be expressed in seconds

- Python has a popular time module which will provide functions that work with time and convert them between the different representations.

- The function time.time() is going to give you the current time on your system in ticks since 12:00 am, January 1, 1970.

Example:

#!/ usr/ bin/ python

Import time; #this is required to include time module

Ticks = time.time()

Print "Number of ticks since 12:00 am, January 1, 1970:", ticks

The outcome will be:

Number of ticks since 12:00am, January 1, 1970: 7186862.733399

- The date arithmetic is going to be easiest to do with ticks.

- The dates before the epoch are not going to be represented in tick form.

- Dates in the far future cannot be represented in this way either. The cutoff point is going to be in 2038.

What is a TimeTuple?

- Python's time functions are going to be handled as a tuple that has nine numbers.

- 0 4 digit year

- 1 month

- 2 day

- 3 hour

- 4 minute

- 5 second

- 6 day of the week

- 7 day of the year

- 8 daylight savings time

- The tuple is going to be equivalent to the struct_time structure.

- 0 tm_year

- 1 tm_mon

- 2 tm_mday

- 3 tm_hour

- 4 tm_min

- 5 tm_sec

- 6 tm_wday

- 7 tm_yday

- 8 tm_isdst

Current time

- You can get a time instant from the seconds since the epoch value into a time tuple

- You will pass the floating point value to the function to get a return of a time tuple that has all nine items in it and they will all be valid.

Example:

#!/ usr/ bin/python

Import time;

Localtime = time.localtime(time.time())

Print "Local current time :", localtime

Your outcome is going to be:

Local current time : time.struct_time(tm_year = 2013, tm_mon = 7,

Tm_mday = 17, tm_hour = 21, tm_min = 26, tm_sec = 3, tm_wday = 2 tm_yday = 198, tm_isdst = 0)

Formatted time

- Time can be formatted as you want it to appear.

- The simplest method is going to be to get time in a readable format

Example:

#!/usr/bin/python

Import time;

Localtime = time.asctime (time. Localtime(time.time()))

Print "local current time :" , localtime

The output will be:

Local current time: Sat. Oct 22 12:21:48 2016

Getting calendar for a month

- The calendar module will provide a wide range of methods that are going to display the year and month.

Example:

#!/usr/bin/python

Import calendar

Cal = calendar. Month (2016, 10)

Print "Her is the calendar:"

Print cal

- The output is going to be the entire calendar for that month.

Time Module

- The time module in Python is going to provide functions for working with the different time and converting them between the representations

Time Functions

- Time.altzone: the offset of the DST time zone

- Time.asctime([tupletime]): the time tuple is going to be accepted and then returned in a readable 24 character string

- Time.clock( ): the current CPU time is going to be retuned as a floating-point number of seconds

- Time.ctime([secs]): is the same function as asctime(localtime(secs)) without any arguments

- Time.mktime(tupletime): an instant expression of the time tuple in local time with a return of floating point values

- Time.sleep(secs): the calling thread for sec seconds will be suspended

- Time.strftime(fmt [, tupletime]): an instant expression is accepted as a time tuple for local time and a string will be returned that represents the instant as a specified by string fmt.

- Time.strptim(str,fmt = '%a %b %d %H: %M: %S %Y'): parses str according to the format and returns the instant in time tuple format.

- Time.time( ): the current time will be returned in an instant as a floating point number of seconds

- Time.tzset(): the time conversion rule will be reset to the ones used by library routines.

Calendar Module

- Calendar.calendar(year, w=2, l=1, c=6): a multiline string is going to be returned with the calendar for years. The year will be formatted into three columns that are separated by c spaces. W will be the width in characters of every day and each line is going to have a length.

- Calendar.fisrtweekday( ): the current settings will be returned for the weekday that begins every week. by default, this will start the week on Monday.

- Calendar.isleap(year): if the year is a leap year, then the condition is going to be true. If it is not a leap year, then it will be returned false.

- Calendar.leapdays(y1, y2): the total number of leap days in the year

- 1Calendar.month(year, month, w=2 l=1): the multiline string with a calendar for month month of year year. There will be one line per week with two header lines.

- Calendar.monthcalendar(year, month): the first two integers are going to be returned. The first is going to be the weekday of the first day for the month the second will be the number of days in the month.

- Calendar.prcal(year, w=2, l=1, c=6): the calendar will be printed with the function calendar.month(year, month, w, l)

- Calendar.setfirstweekday(weekday): the first day of every week will be set.

- Calendar.timegm(tupletime): the inverse for the function time.gmtime will accept the time instant in the time tuple form while returning the same instant like a floating point number of seconds.

- Calendar.weekday(year, month, day): the weekday code will be returned for the given date.

Chapter Sixteen: Python Files I/O

Printing to the Screen

- In order to produce a simple output is to use the print statement so that you can pass zero or be other expressions that are separated by commas.

- The function is going to convert the expressions that you put into the string

Example:

#!/usr/bin/python

Print "Python is a really great language," , "isn't it?"

The output will be: Python is a really great language, isn't it?

Keyboard Input

- Python has two functions that are built into it so that it can read the lines of text from the standard input. This is going to be defaulted by the keyboard. The functions are:

- o Input

- o Raw_input

Raw_input

- Raw_input([prompt]) is going to read one line of input and return it as a string.

Example:

#!/usr/bin/python

Str = raw_input ("Enter your input: ");

Pring "Received input is : " , str

- The prompt that you place in a string is going to display the same string on the screen.

Input

- Input([promt]) is going to be equal to the raw_input function. The only difference is that it will assume the input as a valid

Python expression and return the result evaluated to the user.

Example:

#!/usr/bin/python

Str = input ("Enter your input: ");

Print "Received input is :", str

The output for the code inputted will be:

Enter your input: [x&5 for x in range (2, 10, 2)

Received input is : [10, 20, 30, 40]

Opening and Closing Files

- You have been reading the standard input and output up to this point. From here on in, you are going to be able to see how you can use actual data files.

- Python has basic functions and methods that are going to help in manipulating files by default.

- Most of the file manipulation can be used with a file object.

The Open Function

- To read or write a file you are obviously going to have to open it. To do this, you are going to use Python's open() function.

- This function will create the file object so that it can be utilized to call other methods that are supported and associated with it.

Example:

File object = open(file_name [, access_mode] [, buffering])

Parameter Details

- Buffering: the buffer value is going to be zero. No buffering is going to happen. If the buffer value happens to be one, then a line buffer is going to be performed across the entire file. If you happen to specify the buffer value, with an integer that is great than one, the buffer action is going to be performed with the indicated buffer size. If the buffer size is negative, then the system is going to default to the default behavior.

- File_name: the file_name argument is going to be a string value that has the name of the file that you wish to open.

- Access_mode: the access_mode is going to determine the mode that the file will be opened.

Modes for Opening Files

- R: opens the file for reading only.

- Rb: opens a file for reading but only in the binary format

- R+: the file will be opened for both reading and writing.

- Rb+: the file will be opened for reading and writing in binary code.

- W: the file will be opened for writing only

- Wb: the file will be opened for writing in binary format

- W+: the file is opened for both writing and reading

- Wb+: the fle will be opened for writing and reading in binary code.

- A: the file is opened for appending.

- Ab: the file is opened for appending in binary format

- A+: the file is opened for appending and reading.

- Ab+: the file is opened for appending and reading in binary code.

File Object Attributes

- After a file is opened, there will be a file object that allows you to get information that is related to the file.

Attributes

- File.softspace: the return will be false should the space that is needed for print be true.

- File.closed: the condition will be true if the file is closed.

- File.name: the name of the file will be returned.

File.modeL the return will access the mode that was used to open the file.

Example:

#!/usr/bin/python

#open a file

Fo = open("foo.text", "wb")

Print "Name of the file : ", fo.name

Print "Closed or not : " , fo.closed

Print "Opening mode : ", fo.mode

Print "Softspace flag : " , fo.softspace

The output will be:

Name of the file: foo.txt

Closed or not: false

Opening mode: wb

Softspace flag: 0

Close() Method

- The close() method will flush any information that has been unwritten and close the file so that no more writing can be done.

- Python is going to automatically close the file when the reference object is reassigned.

- It is recommended that you use the close() method in order to close your files.

Syntax:

Fileobject.close()

Example:

#!/usr/bin/python

Open a file

Fo = open("foo.txt", "wb")

Print "Name of the file: ", fo.name

Close opened file

Fo.close()

The result will be:

Name of the file: foo.txt

Reading and Writing Files

- File objects are going to provide access methods

- The read() and write() methods are used to read and write files

Write() Method

- The write() method is going to write a string into an open file.

- Make note that Python strings are going to not just be text, they can be binary data as well.

- The write() method will not add new line characters to the end of the strings.

Syntax:

Fileobject.write(string)

Example:

```
#!/usr/bin/python
```

\# Open a file

Fo = open("foo.txt", "wb")

Fo.write ("Python is a great language. \nYeah its great!! \n");

\# Close opened file

Fo.close()

- A file has been created and given access to write in that file. Once the file is opened again, it is going to have an output like this:

Python is a great language

Yeah its great!!

Read() Method

- The read method will read a string from the opened file.

Syntax:

Fileobject.read([count]);

- The parameter will be the number of bytes that have to be read from the file that has been opened.

- This method will begin reading at the beginning and if the count is missing then it is going to attempt to read as much as it can.

Example:

#!/usr/bin/python

Open a file

Fo = open("foo.txt", "rt")

Str = fo.read(10);

Print "Read String is : " , str

Close opened file

Fo.close()

The result will be:

Read String is: Python is.

File Position

- The tell() method will tell you the current position that you are at in the fle.

- The next read or write is going to occur at that number of bytes from the top of the file.

- The seek(offset[, from]) is going to change the file position.

- An offset argument is going to indicate how many bytes need to be moved.

- The from argument will specify the reference position from where the bytes have been moved.

- Should the from be set to zero, the beginning file is going to reference the position and one will mean that the current position is going to be the reference position.

- If it is at two, then the end of the file is going to be the reference position.

Example:

```
#!/usr/bin/python

# Open a file

Fo = open(" foo.txt", "rt")

Str = fo.read(10);

Print "Read String is : ", str

# Check current position

Position = fo.tell();

Print "Curren file position : ", positon

#Reposition pointer at the beginning once again

Position = fo.see (0,0);

Str = fo.read(10);

Print "Again read String is : ", str

# Close Opened file

Fo.close()
```

The result produced shall be:

Read String is : Python is

Current file position : 10

Again read String is : Python is

Renaming and Deleting Files

- The os module will provide various methods to assist in performing file processing operations

- This module is going to need to be imported first before you call any related functions

Rename() Method

- Two arguments will be taken and the current file name as well as the new file name.

Syntax:

Os.rename(current_file_name, new_file_name)

Example:

#!/usr/bin/python

Import os

Rename a file from test1.txt to test2.txt

Os.rename("test1.txt", "test2.txt")

Remove() Method

- The remove method is going to delete files through the use of the file name so that the argument can be deleted.

Syntax

Os.remove(file_name)

Example:

#!/usr/bin/python

Import os

Delete file test2.txt

Os.remove("text2.txt")

Dictionaries in Python

- All files are going to be contained into varies dictionaries

- Python has no problems handling these

- The os module has several methods to aid in the creation, removal, and changing of dictionaries

Mkdir() Method:

- The mkdir() method is a os module that creates dictionaries within the current directory.

- It is your job to supply the argument when using this method.

- The argument needs to contain the name of the directory that you wish to create.

Syntax:

Os.mkdir("newdir")

Example:

#!/usr/bin/python

Import os

Changing a directory to "/home/newdir"

Os.chdir ("/home/newdir")

Getcwd() Method

- This method is going to display the dictionary that is currently working

syntax:

os.getcwd()

example:

#!/usr/bin/python

Import os

This would give location of the current directory

Os.getcwd()

Rmdir() Method

- This method can delete the directory so that an argument can be passed in this method.

- Before you remove the directory, all of the contents should be removed.

Syntax:

Os.rmdir('dirname')

Example:

#!/usr/bin/python

Import os

This would remove "/tmp/test" directory

Os.rmdir ("/tmp/test")

File and directory methods

- Three important sourced will provide a wide range of utility methods that can be used to handle and manipulate files and directories depending on your operating system.

- File object method: the file is going to provide the functions needed to manipulate files

- OS object methodS: the methods needed will be provided so that files can be processed along with directories.

Chapter Seventeen:
Useful Python Codes

- There are some codes that you are going to find useful when you are using Python.

- These codes are going to be ones that you are going to use often in your coding progress.

- It is advised that you keep these codes somewhere that is easily accessible.

- **Unpacking:**

```
>>> a, b, c = 1, 2, 3

>>> a, b, c

(1, 2, 3)

>>> a, b, c = [1, 2, 3]

>>> a, b, c

(1, 2, 3)

>>> a, b, c = (2 * i + 1 for i in range(3))

>>> a, b, c

(1, 3, 5)
```

```
>>> a, (b, c), d = [1, (2, 3), 4]
>>> a
1
>>> b
2
>>> c
3
>>> d
4
```

- **Unpacking for swapping variables:**

```
>>> a, b = 1, 2
>>> a, b = b, a
>>> a, b
(2, 1)
```

- **Extended unpacking (use in Python 3 only)**

```
>>> a, *b, c = [1, 2, 3, 4, 5]
>>> a
1
>>> b
[2, 3, 4]
>>> c
5
```

- **Negative indexing**

```
>>> a = [0, 1, 2, 3, 4, 5, 6, 7, 8, 9, 10]
>>> a[-1]
10
>>> a[-3]
8
```

- **List slices (a[start: end])**

>>> a = [0, 1, 2, 3, 4, 5, 6, 7, 8, 9, 10]

>>> a[2:8]

[2, 3, 4, 5, 6, 7]

- **List Slices with Negative Indexing**

>>> a = [0, 1, 2, 3, 4, 5, 6, 7, 8, 9, 10]

>>> a[-4:-2]

[7, 8]

- **List Slices with Step (a[start: end: step])**

>>> a = [0, 1, 2, 3, 4, 5, 6, 7, 8, 9, 10]

>>> a[::2]

[0, 2, 4, 6, 8, 10]

>>> a[::3]

[0, 3, 6, 9]

```
>>> a[2:8:2]

[2, 4, 6]
```

- **List Slices with negative step**

```
>>> a = [0, 1, 2, 3, 4, 5, 6, 7, 8, 9, 10]

>>> a[::-1]

[10, 9, 8, 7, 6, 5, 4, 3, 2, 1, 0]

>>> a[::-2]

[10, 8, 6, 4, 2, 0]
```

- **List Slice Assignment**

```
>>> a = [1, 2, 3, 4, 5]

>>> a[2:3] = [0, 0]

>>> a

[1, 2, 0, 0, 4, 5]

>>> a[1:1] = [8, 9]

>>> a
```

[1, 8, 9, 2, 0, 0, 4, 5]

>>> a[1:-1] = []

>>> a

[1, 5]

- **Naming Slices (slice(start, end, step))**

>>> a = [0, 1, 2, 3, 4, 5]

>>> LASTTHREE = slice(-3, None)

>>> LASTTHREE

slice(-3, None, None)

>>> a[LASTTHREE]

[3, 4, 5]

- **Iterating over list index and value pairs (enumerate)**

>>> a = ['Hello', 'world', '!']

>>> for i, x in enumerate(a):

```
...    print '{}: {}'.format(i, x)

...

0: Hello

1: world

2: !
```

- **Iterating over dictionary key and value pairs (dict.iteritems)**

```
>>> m = {'a': 1, 'b': 2, 'c': 3, 'd': 4}

>>> for k, v in m.iteritems():

...    print '{}: {}'.format(k, v)

...

a: 1

c: 3

b: 2

d: 4
```

• Zipping and unzipping lists and iterables

>>> a = [1, 2, 3]

>>> b = ['a', 'b', 'c']

>>> z = zip(a, b)

>>> z

[(1, 'a'), (2, 'b'), (3, 'c')]

>>> zip(*z)

[(1, 2, 3), ('a', 'b', 'c')]

• Grouping adjacent list items using zip

>>> a = [1, 2, 3, 4, 5, 6]

>>> # Using iterators

>>> group_adjacent = lambda a, k: zip(*([iter(a)] * k))

>>> group_adjacent(a, 3)

[(1, 2, 3), (4, 5, 6)]

```
>>> group_adjacent(a, 2)

[(1, 2), (3, 4), (5, 6)]

>>> group_adjacent(a, 1)

[(1,), (2,), (3,), (4,), (5,), (6,)]


>>> # Using slices

>>> from itertools import islice

>>> group_adjacent = lambda a, k: zip(*(islice(a, i, None, k) for i in range(k)))

>>> group_adjacent(a, 3)

[(1, 2, 3), (4, 5, 6)]

>>> group_adjacent(a, 2)

[(1, 2), (3, 4), (5, 6)]

>>> group_adjacent(a, 1)

[(1,), (2,), (3,), (4,), (5,), (6,)]
```

- **Sliding windows (n-grams) using zip and iterators**

```
>>> from itertools import islice

>>> def n_grams(a, n):

...    z = (islice(a, i, None) for i in range(n))

...    return zip(*z)

...

>>> a = [1, 2, 3, 4, 5, 6]

>>> n_grams(a, 3)

[(1, 2, 3), (2, 3, 4), (3, 4, 5), (4, 5, 6)]

>>> n_grams(a, 2)

[(1, 2), (2, 3), (3, 4), (4, 5), (5, 6)]

>>> n_grams(a, 4)

[(1, 2, 3, 4), (2, 3, 4, 5), (3, 4, 5, 6)]
```

- **Inverting a dictionary using zip**

```
>>> m = {'a': 1, 'b': 2, 'c': 3, 'd': 4}
>>> m.items()
[('a', 1), ('c', 3), ('b', 2), ('d', 4)]
>>> zip(m.values(), m.keys())
[(1, 'a'), (3, 'c'), (2, 'b'), (4, 'd')]
>>> mi = dict(zip(m.values(), m.keys()))
>>> mi
{1: 'a', 2: 'b', 3: 'c', 4: 'd'}
```

- **Flattening lists**

```
>>> a = [[1, 2], [3, 4], [5, 6]]
>>> list(itertools.chain.from_iterable(a))
[1, 2, 3, 4, 5, 6]
```

```
>>> sum(a, [])
[1, 2, 3, 4, 5, 6]
```

```
>>> [x for l in a for x in l]

[1, 2, 3, 4, 5, 6]


>>> a = [[[1, 2], [3, 4]], [[5, 6], [7, 8]]]

>>> [x for l1 in a for l2 in l1 for x in l2]

[1, 2, 3, 4, 5, 6, 7, 8]


>>> a = [1, 2, [3, 4], [[5, 6], [7, 8]]]

>>> flatten = lambda x: [y for l in x for y in
flatten(l)] if type(x) is list else [x]

>>> flatten(a)

[1, 2, 3, 4, 5, 6, 7, 8]
```

- **Generator expressions**

```
>>> g = (x ** 2 for x in xrange(10))
>>> next(g)
0
>>> next(g)
1
>>> next(g)
4
>>> next(g)
9
>>> sum(x ** 3 for x in xrange(10))
2025
>>> sum(x ** 3 for x in xrange(10) if x % 3 == 1)
408
```

- **Dictionary comprehensions**

```
>>> m = {x: x ** 2 for x in range(5)}

>>> m

{0: 0, 1: 1, 2: 4, 3: 9, 4: 16}


>>> m = {x: 'A' + str(x) for x in range(10)}

>>> m

{0: 'A0', 1: 'A1', 2: 'A2', 3: 'A3', 4: 'A4', 5: 'A5', 6: 'A6', 7: 'A7', 8: 'A8', 9: 'A9'}
```

- **Inverting a dictionary using a dictionary comprehension**

```
>>> m = {'a': 1, 'b': 2, 'c': 3, 'd': 4}

>>> m

{'d': 4, 'a': 1, 'b': 2, 'c': 3}

>>> {v: k for k, v in m.items()}

{1: 'a', 2: 'b', 3: 'c', 4: 'd'}
```

- **Named tuples (collections . namedtuple)**

```
>>> Point = collections.namedtuple('Point', ['x', 'y'])

>>> p = Point(x=1.0, y=2.0)

>>> p

Point(x=1.0, y=2.0)

>>> p.x

1.0

>>> p.w

2.0
```

- **Inheriting from named tuples**

```
>>> class Point(collections.namedtuple('PointBase', ['x', 'y'])):

...     __slots__ = ()

...     def __add__(self, other):
```

```
...            return Point(x=self.x + other.x, y=self.y
+ other.y)

...

>>> p = Point(x=1.0, y=2.0)

>>> q = Point(x=2.0, y=3.0)

>>> p + q

Point(x=3.0, y=5.0)
```

- **Sets and set operations**

```
>>> A = {1, 2, 3, 3}

>>> A

set([1, 2, 3])

>>> B = {3, 4, 5, 6, 7}

>>> B

set([3, 4, 5, 6, 7])

>>> A | B

set([1, 2, 3, 4, 5, 6, 7])
```

```
>>> A & B

set([3])

>>> A - B

set([1, 2])

>>> B - A

set([4, 5, 6, 7])

>>> A ^ B

set([1, 2, 4, 5, 6, 7])

>>> (A ^ B) == ((A - B) | (B - A))

True
```

- **Multisets and multiset operations (collections.counter)**

```
>>> A = collections.Counter([1, 2, 2])

>>> B = collections.Counter([2, 2, 3])

>>> A

Counter({2: 2, 1: 1})
```

```
>>> B

Counter({2: 2, 3: 1})

>>> A | B

Counter({2: 2, 1: 1, 3: 1})

>>> A & B

Counter({2: 2})

>>> A + B

Counter({2: 4, 1: 1, 3: 1})

>>> A - B

Counter({1: 1})

>>> B - A

Counter({3: 1})
```

- **Most common elements in an iterable (collections.counter)**

```
>>> A = collections.Counter([1, 1, 2, 2, 3, 3, 3, 3, 4, 5, 6, 7])

>>> A

Counter({3: 4, 1: 2, 2: 2, 4: 1, 5: 1, 6: 1, 7: 1})

>>> A.most_common(1)

[(3, 4)]

>>> A.most_common(3)

[(3, 4), (1, 2), (2, 2)]
```

- **Double ended queue (collections.deque)**

```
>>> Q = collections.deque()

>>> Q.append(1)

>>> Q.appendleft(2)

>>> Q.extend([3, 4])

>>> Q.extendleft([5, 6])
```

```
>>> Q
deque([6, 5, 2, 1, 3, 4])
>>> Q.pop()
4
>>> Q.popleft()
6
>>> Q
deque([5, 2, 1, 3])
>>> Q.rotate(3)
>>> Q
deque([2, 1, 3, 5])
>>> Q.rotate(-3)
>>> Q
deque([5, 2, 1, 3])
```

- **Double ended queue with maximum length (collections.deque)**

```
>>> last_three = collections.deque(maxlen=3)

>>> for i in xrange(10):

...     last_three.append(i)

...     print ', '.join(str(x) for x in last_three)

...

0

0, 1

0, 1, 2

1, 2, 3

2, 3, 4

3, 4, 5

4, 5, 6

5, 6, 7

6, 7, 8

7, 8, 9
```

- **Ordered dictionaries (collections.OrderedDict)**

```
>>> m = dict((str(x), x) for x in range(10))
```

```
>>> print ', '.join(m.keys())
```

1, 0, 3, 2, 5, 4, 7, 6, 9, 8

```
>>> m = collections.OrderedDict((str(x), x) for x in range(10))
```

```
>>> print ', '.join(m.keys())
```

0, 1, 2, 3, 4, 5, 6, 7, 8, 9

```
>>> m = collections.OrderedDict((str(x), x) for x in range(10, 0, -1))
```

```
>>> print ', '.join(m.keys())
```

10, 9, 8, 7, 6, 5, 4, 3, 2, 1

- **Default dictionaries (collections.defaultdict)**

```
>>> m = dict()

>>> m['a']

Traceback (most recent call last):

  File "<stdin>", line 1, in <module>

KeyError: 'a'

>>>

>>> m = collections.defaultdict(int)

>>> m['a']

0

>>> m['b']

0

>>> m = collections.defaultdict(str)

>>> m['a']

''

>>> m['b'] += 'a'
```

```
>>> m['b']
```

'a'

```
>>> m = collections.defaultdict(lambda:
'[default value]')
```

```
>>> m['a']
```

'[default value]'

```
>>> m['b']
```

'[default value]'

- **Using default dictionaries to represent simple trees**

```
>>> import json
```

```
>>> tree = lambda: collections.defaultdict(tree)
```

```
>>> root = tree()
```

```
>>> root['menu']['id'] = 'file'
```

```
>>> root['menu']['value'] = 'File'
```

```
>>> root['menu']['menuitems']['new']['value'] =
'New'
```

```
>>> root['menu']['menuitems']['new']['onclick']
= 'new();'

>>> root['menu']['menuitems']['open']['value'] =
'Open'

>>> root['menu']['menuitems']['open']['onclick']
= 'open();'

>>> root['menu']['menuitems']['close']['value'] =
'Close'

>>> root['menu']['menuitems']['close']['onclick']
= 'close();'

>>> print json.dumps(root, sort_keys=True,
indent=4, separators=(',', ': '))
{
    "menu": {
        "id": "file",
        "menuitems": {
            "close": {
                "onclick": "close();",
                "value": "Close"
            },
```

```
      "new": {

         "onclick": "new();",

         "value": "New"

      },

      "open": {

         "onclick": "open();",

         "value": "Open"

      }

   },

   "value": "File"

  }

}
```

- **Mapping objects to unique counting numbers (collections.defaultdict)**

```
>>> import itertools, collections
```

```
>>> value_to_numeric_map =
collections.defaultdict(itertools.count().next)
```

```
>>> value_to_numeric_map['a']
```

```
0
```

```
>>> value_to_numeric_map['b']
```

```
1
```

```
>>> value_to_numeric_map['c']
```

```
2
```

```
>>> value_to_numeric_map['a']
```

```
0
```

```
>>> value_to_numeric_map['b']
```

```
1
```

- **Largest and smallest elements (heapq.nlargest and heapq.nsmallest)**

```
>>> a = [random.randint(0, 100) for __ in xrange(100)]

>>> heapq.nsmallest(5, a)

[3, 3, 5, 6, 8]

>>> heapq.nlargest(5, a)

[100, 100, 99, 98, 98]
```

- **Cartesian products (itertools.product)**

```
>>> for p in itertools.product([1, 2, 3], [4, 5]):

(1, 4)

(1, 5)

(2, 4)

(2, 5)

(3, 4)

(3, 5)

>>> for p in itertools.product([0, 1], repeat=4):
```

```
...     print ''.join(str(x) for x in p)
...
```

0000

0001

0010

0011

0100

0101

0110

0111

1000

1001

1010

1011

1100

1101

1110

1111

Conclusion

Thank you again for purchasing this book! It was greatly appreciated.

I hope this book was able to provide you with the basics of Python and how you can use it in order to further your work experience so that you can move up in your job or even get a better job.

The next step is to download Python and the programs that are associated with it and try out some of what you learned in this book. It is not going to be easy at first, but the more that you practice, the easier it is going to become. Do not give up faith if you do not get the coding on the first try.

Additionally, please visit our Amazon Author page for more great info and resources.

You will find all the books you need to learn about:

Python Programming, SQL, JavaScript, and even **TOR** if that's something you fancy!!

Last but not least, if you enjoyed this book and thought it was helpful, we certainly won't say no to a 5-star **review on Amazon**.

Thank You and Best of Luck in Your Python Programming Endeavors!!!

www.ingramcontent.com/pod-product-compliance
Lightning Source LLC
Chambersburg PA
CBHW071128050326
40690CB00008B/1374